Choose a topic and start to practise writing. Each k
to help you start to write…stories, reports, articles,
more. Start collecting them now.

Guinea Pig creative writing booklets also provide extra practice for
children who have completed:

- Creative Story Writing ISBN: 9780955831508
- Persuasive Writing & Argument ISBN: 9780955831515
- Information Writing ISBN: 9780955831522

They are for:

* children who are working at Key Stage 2 of the National Curriculum,
  levels 3-5 (in Years 5 and 6 of primary school),
* children who are working at Key Stage 3, levels 3-5 (Years 7 and 8 of
  Secondary School).

They provide practice for all 9-13 year olds, especially children taking
11+ examinations.

© **Copyright 2011**

**This pack may not under any circumstances be
photocopied, without the prior consent of the publisher.**

Written by Sally A Jones and Amanda C Jones

Published by GUINEA PIG EDUCATION

2 Cobs Way,
New Haw,
Addlestone,
Surrey,
KT15 3AF.

www.guineapigeducation.co.uk

Let's **learn** to *write* <u>non-fiction</u>.

When you *write non-fiction*, **<u>you may write</u>**:

- an article

- a leaflet

- a diary

- a description.

> - *A description may describe the way people look, dress, their character, attitudes and abilities.*
> - *A description may describe the way a place looks.*
> - *A description may describe the way something feels, tastes and smells.*

<u>You must decide</u>:

1. Who will be my target audience?

2. Who will read this writing?

3. What is the purpose of my writing?

4. Am I aiming to give somebody a picture of something I have experienced?

5. Am I using my senses to impact the reader- seeing, hearing, feeling, touching, tasting?

<u>Use imagery or figurative language:</u>

Metaphors - *'you're an angel' means you are a good person.*

Similes - *'as white as snow'*

Personification - *'the wind whispered softly in the trees.'*

Admirable adjectives and nouns - *'delicious cake.'*

Powerful verbs and adverbs - *'gobbled greedily.'*

When you write to **describe**:

PARAGRAPH 1 • Write an introduction to set the scene. • Have a colourful opening to get the attention of the reader.	**Remember:** • Use powerful words - verbs, adverbs, nouns and adjectives. • Use similes and metaphors.
PARAGRAPH 2, 3, 4... • Write about each part of this experience in separate paragraphs in chronological order.	• Use connectives or conjunctions: - *and or but (to join compound sentences)* - *or, so, if, when, while, after, before, because, unless, until, whereas, although (to join complex sentences)* - *use pronouns - who, which, whose, what, that* - *to link ideas use - firstly, later, therefore, on the other hand, at that moment, by this time, next, soon...* • Use a range of sentences – simple, compound and complex sentences
Conclusion • Draw all your ideas together in a conclusion.	• Make personal comments

It is half term and you are out shopping with your mum. As you pass the coffee shop, you see the ***yummiest* cake** you have ever seen… <u>You want to eat it!</u>

What is a cup cake?

A cup cake is a sponge cake in a brightly coloured bun case, covered in thick cream and sprinkled with sugar decorations or sweets and maybe with a cherry on top.

The Cup Cake

It was almost eleven o'clock when we passed the coffee shop. Mum and I had been shopping for ages. My legs were starting to ache and we were both really thirsty. The smell of hot roasted coffee drifted out of the shop and wafted into our nostrils. I pressed my nose up against the glass window and peered in at the plates piled high with pastries. Then, I saw the yummiest cakes I had ever seen. They were cup cakes covered in pale yellow icing, sprinkled with edible glitter and jellied sweets.
"Can I have one of those," I begged my mum.

We entered the crowded coffee shop; the pungent smell of coffee overpowered me.
"Hello," smiled the assistant sweetly, "what can I get for you?"
"A cappuccino for me," replied mum. "What would you like Becky?"
"I'll have a lemonade please and one of those cup cakes..." Mum paused and mumbled that granny was cooking lunch. I looked persuasively at her.
"Please mum…please…." She hesitated, in what for me felt like an agonising second. The assistant stood poised with the tongs.
"…OK, we'll have one of those cakes as well." The tongs descended onto the cup cake. The assistant took the money and passed us the tray
"Enjoy!" she said. The cake sat triumphantly on its plate as I carried it carefully to an empty table and sat down.

The café was buzzing as people chatted together. In the background, I could hear the sound of knives and forks scraping together and babies crying... but my attention was only on the delicious, creamy cup cake that was right in front of me. I observed its swirling primrose cream, twirled up to form a tall peak, that was drizzled with sugar coated candies shaped like stars. The sweet aroma of icing was drifting up to my nose. It was making my mouth water. How could I take a bite into this? It looks too good to eat.

Mum joined me at the table. Looking at her watch, she uttered,
"Eat up quickly." Eagerly, I picked up the delicious delicacy and peeled back the brightly coloured bun case. Filled with anticipation, I lifted the tempting cake to my lips and took a big bite into the soft sponge. I licked off the sweet icing that was dripping down the side and crunched up the candies. It was superb. It was the yummiest cake I had ever tasted but, before I knew it, it was gone.
"Did you enjoy that?" mum said, as she gulped her coffee down and prepared to stand up.
"It was the yummiest, most scrumptious cake I've ever tasted. The only problem: it was too small and I would quite like another one." I took a few sips of my lemonade, but... Mum stood up and moved towards the door promptly. I decided that when I saw Dad next week, I would bring him to this café.

You enter a café and see a cake. Describe the cake you have chosen, how you bought it and what it tasted like.

Use these questions to help you.

You see a café.

- Look in the window.
- Press your face up against the glass.
- What do you see for sale?
- Describe it.
- What do you say to your mum/ dad/ aunt?

You are in the café.

- You stand by the counter.
- A café assistant serves you.
- Write the dialogue.
- What is it like in the café?
- What noises and smells are there?
- What did you choose?
- How do you feel?

Use your senses to describe how you eat the cake:

- What does it look like?
- What does it smell like?
- What does it taste like?
- How does it feel in your mouth?
- Describe the experience.
- How do you feel when it's eaten?
- What do you say to your mum/dad/aunt?
- Would you like another one?

Before you start to write, you may like to look at the writing tips and techniques at the back of the book.

Now write the story you planned.

Write down a recipe to make some cup cakes. Put the instructions in order.

To make 24 cup cakes you will need:

- 100g self raising flour
- 100g of castor sugar
- 100g of margarine
- 2 eggs
- 100g of icing sugar
- food colouring
- jelly sweets
- sugar sprinkles

To make 12 halve the ingredients.

You will need to ask an adult to help you do work in the kitchen.

Which *order* do you think these instructions should go in?

- **Mix** the icing sugar and butter together with a few drops of food colouring and stir until it looks like thick cream. If it stands in peaks you can pipe it with a piping bag and nozzle.

- **Spoon** the mixture into some cup cake cases.

- Now **beat** in 2 eggs.

- **Put** the icing on the buns and sprinkle on some sweets.

- **Sift** in the flour and stir it until the mixture is mixed together thoroughly.

- **Get** an adult to put the cupcakes in the oven at 180°C for 15 minutes.

- **Beat** the margarine and sugar together in a bowl until soft.

- **Enjoy**.

Check your answer

Beat the margarine and sugar together in a bowl until soft. Now beat in 2 eggs. Sift in the flour and stir it until the mixture is mixed together thoroughly. Spoon the mixture into some cup cake cases. Get an adult to put them in to the oven at 180 c for 15 minutes. Mix the icing sugar and butter together with a few drops of food colouring and stir until it looks like thick cream. Put the icing on the buns and sprinkle on some sweets. Enjoy.

Now, write the story about the day I made cup cakes.

Make a new paragraph for each part of the experience.

(1)   <u>Shopping for the ingredients</u>:

- going to the supermarket
- choosing the ingredients
- bringing them home

(2)   <u>Making the cakes in the kitchen</u>:

- Getting out utensils
- Do you spill the mixture?
- Do they go wrong?
- Are they too flat, too tall, too burnt, not cooked, too crumbly?

(3)   <u>Serving them up for tea</u>:

- What do they look like?
- How do they taste, feel and smell?
- What do people think of them?

Now write the story you planned.

Moving the story on:

Let's imagine...

It is a special celebration. You sit down to eat. Someone has made a plate of dainty, delectable delicacies – cupcakes. Crinkly blue wax paper cases are filled with soft sponge. On top, there is a swirling mass of frosted blue icing, made to look like waves. Each cake has a character, from under the sea that has been intricately moulded in icing. Every detail has been cut from candy. But what happens when you try to eat these amazing creations? Let's try them...

As the soft, blue butter cream slithered down my throat, it tasted as sweet as honey, but I started to feel a strange sensation come over me. I was shrinking down in size and when I came to my senses, I was in a different place. There was something strange about the ground beneath my feet. I was walking on a soft, squelchy substance... slip sliding along. Where was I? I surveyed the scene around me. There were nine little blue pools and the water was swirled up into little peaks like waves.

I must explore while I'm here I thought and paddled through the creamy waves. I leapt from one pool to another and soon came to some fish like shapes, swimming through the blue sea. I don't know what came over me, but I put out my hands to grab one. It lay in my palm, like a red gummy fruit sweet. It smelt so fruity, so sweet, that I took a little lick and then put it in my mouth, swallowing it down in one gulp. Delicious!

I was about to reach for another when I saw something that made my blood freeze. It was a black eye, the size of a chocolate chip, and it stared at me ominously. I saw, the creature's immense black body. I saw his open mouth full of razor sharp teeth and I knew he was ready to launch himself out of the swirling blue waters and gulp me down in one mouthful. "Help!" I screamed. I summoned all my strength and took a huge leap...

I landed with a splash in the next pool, but here, too, hideous creatures lurked – squid and octopus dangling their terrifying tentacles. Filled with terror, I jumped from pool to pool...

Eventually, I sought refuge under some rocks. It was a silent secret place, where sea horses floated, where sea urchins hid amongst the sweet smelling shells, where anemone and molluscs clung to the rocks. I waited in the tangled, green weed, listening to the roar of the ocean. What was that sound of singing? It was soothing; it was lulling me to sleep. At that moment, I became aware that I was not alone. A pair of blue eyes met mine and peered at me with such intensity that I stepped back. Then I saw that they belonged to a beautiful girl. She was sat on a stone, combing her long flowing hair, but there was something quite odd about her. She had the tail of a fish but the head of a human. She was half fish and half human. "She's a mer.......mer........mermaid," I thought. She spoke to me in a soft voice, which was only just audible.

"You won't eat us," she insisted. "No one will. It took that baker twelve hours to make us. We are so intricately sculpted by his hand, in such fine detail, but we really belong in the ocean... Come with me, I'll show you my kingdom under the sea. She gripped my hand so tightly I had no choice, but to follow.

End on a cliff hanger. What other ending could there be?

Imagine the **_ocean._**

Describe the scene. Write an awesome description of life under the sea.

Can you think of any more vocabulary?

sea horses	**jelly fish**	octopus
<u>squid</u>	sea urchins	tropical fish
anemone	molluscs	powerful waves
mermaids	<u>sharks</u>	_ship wreck_
underworld	**_seaweed_**	rocks
volcanoes	caves	**dark**
dismal	dingy	mythical creatures Can you name some?

Write your description here.

Now, *imagine* your own *cakes.*

Perhaps your mum made you an alligator cake – forming his body from eighteen sponge cupcakes. His scaly skin is made from smarties, his claws from marzipan, his teeth from marshmallows and his eyes are *Liquorice allsorts*. What happens when you eat him? Do you end up going on a trip to the swampy everglades in Florida U.S.A?

Imagine an underwater world.

It is full of colourful fishes, sea horses and giant squid. Sea monsters lurk in the depths of the ocean. Unexplored caverns under the sea might be the kingdom of strange mythical creatures, yet to be discovered.

Imagine a *follow up* story

(the genre is fantasy, so you can write about things that can't really happen)

What happens to the narrator (story teller) when he or she goes with the mermaid? Write an adventure about under the sea.

(1)　Introduce characters, setting and plot.

- Who...
- Where...
- When...

(2)　Develop plot – complication, problems, tension and suspense.

- What happens to you under the sea?
- Are there any dangers?
- Are you lured into a cave? Are you trapped?
- How do you escape? Who helps you?

(3)　Wind up story with a suitable ending.

- How is the situation resolved?
- How does it end?

Now write this story.

Imagine you find yourself on a huge white cake, decorated with frosted icing and piped with rosettes. There are some wild animals from the arctic on the snow scene – reindeer, polar bears and... What adventure do you have?

....

....

....

....

....

....

....

....

....

....

....

....

....

....

....

....

....

....

....

Try thinking of some other cake adventures...

Maybe your cakes are shaped like...

| clowns | princesses | fairies | lions | cats | dogs | butterflies |
| sharks | flowers | bugs | aliens | bats | wolves | |

Now write a story about what happens when you bite into your cake...

Invite a friend for tea. Remember to set out the letter with correct punctuation. Use the letter below to help you. Becky writes in more detail than is usually required in a birthday invitation. She writes a chatty, informal letter to her friend.

10 Cumberland Court,

Rushford,

RG45 3AG.

10th April.

Dear Kitty,

      Please come to celebrate my special day. I thought we'd have a girl's/boy's night at home, like my mum does with her friends – so don't worry I haven't organized any surprises. No one is coming to do a makeover or try to sell us anything. It'll just be a relaxing evening when we can chat and have fun – watch some exciting DVDs or a bit of Y Factor on TV. You can sleep over and my mum will drop you back at about 11am on Sunday morning.

By the way, if you come, you'll be able to bite into the yummiest chocolate cup cakes you've ever tasted, which I helped mum make. We've decorated them with layers of gooey, chocolate cream and given them characters - of bugs, aliens, bats and wolves. It will be the scariest late night feast ever! Of course, they're all made from candy and they are sure to be delicious. They look amazing on their tiered cake stand. Each one has a candle. I can't wait to blow them out.

Here are some directions to my house - turn right at Fresco's into Station Road. Cumberland Court is on the left, at the far end of the road, opposite Amelia Jane's café. I really hope you can come and look forward to a fantastic evening.

Lots of love,

Becky

Now write a reply from Kitty.

Invite a friend for tea.

Remember to set out the letter with correct punctuation.

Try writing a friendly, informal letter, like the one Becky wrote. It gives more information than the usual letter. Now, try writing it as an e-mail. How different would it be?

<table>
<tr><td colspan="2">New | Reply   Reply all   Foward | Delete   Mark as ▼   Move to ▼</td></tr>
<tr><td>

INBOX (240)

FOLDERS

Junk (109)

Drafts (11)

Sent

Deleted (15)

New Folder

</td><td>

Hi Kitty,

☐ **Kitty**   15/01/2015
    To Kitty@guineapig.co.uk   **Reply**

</td></tr>
</table>

Below are some more informal letters (e-mails), with three paragraphs you can write... Add lots of exciting detail. Include – when, where, at, what you will do and what you need to bring?

Your friend invites you to:

- his or her grandma's caravan. It will be an eighty mile drive in the car and you will have a fish and chip supper. There will also be a fair with a roller coaster.

- shopping at the new mall, followed by a pizza at the fast food place and then a sleep over.

- a bowling and swimming party, followed by burger and chips.

- a firework party at an uncle's house, followed by hot dogs and baked potatoes.

- a football party in the park, followed by a dinner at his or her house.

Can you think of some more?

Now write the replies to the letters.

Think – Why do I want to go? *(it will be fun)*.

Why do you not want to go? *(you are grounded, you don't have a new swimming costume, you do not get on with one of the other guests)*.

Design a *dream* **butter cream cupcake**.

Use the following ideas to help you.

Cup cakes are:

delicious, **scrumptious**, mouth watering, **yummy**, luscious, delectable, gorgeous...

Icing can be:

perfectly smooth, *swirly*, **delicious**, frosty,

Flavour with:

vanilla, *chocolate*, caramel, cappuccino, **mocha**, *mint* and more...

Decorate with:

colourful sugar candies, **silver balls**, hearts, jelly beans, hundreds and thousands, **chocolate buttons**, *chocolate flakes*, yummy chewy sweets, scrumptious marsh marshmallows, *chopped nuts*, **drizzles** and gorgeous treats...

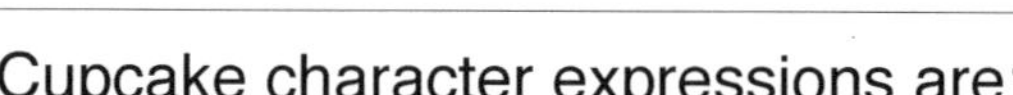

Find some more words by looking in a thesaurus. Write them on this page.

<u>Revise Writing Techniques</u>

When writing your own description of eating cup cakes. Use sound words like:

Onomatopoeia

words that sound like the actual sound.

gulped it down

Alliteration

words that have the same initial sound.

soft sponge, plates piled high

Metaphors

compare a thing, people or ideas by saying it is something else

The café was buzzing.

(Meaning the café was noisy with people talking.)

Similies

compare one thing to another,
using like or as.

as pretty as a picture

Personification

giving human qualities to objects

It seemed to be saying 'don't eat me.' It sat before me on the plate.

Repetition

chewed and chewed

Good adjectives

describing words that go with nouns

scrumptious cake, thick cream

Good verbs

action words

oozed, sprinkled, licked

Good adverbs

go with verbs

promptly, triumphantly

Can you find some examples in the book or make up some of your own.

Made in the USA
Monee, IL
07 July 2026